EARTH'S CHANGING LANDSCAPE

Earthquakes & Volcanoes

Chris Oxlade

W

FRANKLIN WATTS

LONDON•SYDNEY

This edition 2006

Franklin Watts
338 Euston Road
London NW1 3BH

Franklin Watts Australia
Level 17/207 Kent Street
Sydney NSW 2000

Series editor: Sarah Peutrill
Series designer: Simon Borrough
Art director: Jonathan Hair
Picture researcher: Juliet Duff
Illustrations: Ian Thompson
Series consultant: Steve Watts, FRGS, Principal
Lecturer in Geography Education at the University of
Sunderland

A CIP catalogue record for this book is available from the
British Library

ISBN: 978 0 7496 6951 5
Dewey Classification: 551.2

Printed in Malaysia

Picture credits:
James Davis Travel Photography: 15, 23 left, 26.
Eye Ubiquitous: 21 CM Leask; 23 right Laurence Fordyce,
27 Paul Thompson; 28 Paul Seheult. Geoscience Features:
7, 34 top. Holt Studios International: 17 Dick Roberts; 34
bottom Rosie Mayer. Frank Lane Picture Agency: 6, 36, 37.
Photodisc: 20. Science Photo Library: 11 Simon Fraser; 18
Dr Ian Robson; 19 Ray Fairbanks; 41, 43 David Parker; 42
Jeremy Bishop. Still Pictures: 9, 35 Edward Parker; 13 Jose
Kalpers; 16 Martial Aquarone; 24 Steve Kaufman; 25 Nigel
Dickinson; 29 Pierre Gleize; 31 Kevin Schafer; 40 Lineair.
Topfoto: 22, 38, 39. Front Cover: Still Pictures/Otto Hahn.

Every attempt has been made to clear copyright. Should
there be any inadvertent omission, please apply to the
publisher for rectification.

Franklin Watts is a division of Hachette Children's Books

CONTENTS

For most of us the landscape of the Earth's surface seems permanent, solid and safe. But over millions of years the landscape has been changed dramatically by earthquakes and volcanoes. These events have built mountain ranges, created chains of islands and destroyed major cities.

Buildings destroyed by a landslide caused by a massive earthquake in Alaska in 1964.

Unstoppable forces Earthquakes and volcanic eruptions are very different events, but they are closely linked. They are both created by the movement of molten rock and heat deep inside the Earth. Earthquakes and volcanoes are the visible evidence of these subterranean movements.

Follow it through: subterranean movement

Movement of molten rock inside the Earth

Earthquakes shake the Earth

Volcanoes erupt

Effects on the landscape

Most earthquakes and volcanoes affect only a relatively small part of the landscape. On a local scale they are very dramatic events, but on a global scale they are minor. However, over millions of years the subterranean movements that cause earthquakes and volcanoes have changed the appearance of the whole planet.

Earthquakes cause the ground to shake. In most cases when the shaking stops the landscape is left unchanged, but strong earthquakes can crack the ground, set off landslides and mudslides, create huge waves at sea, and knock down buildings.

Volcanoes have a greater effect on the landscape than earthquakes. Much of the Earth's surface is covered with rock from volcanoes. They build mountains and islands thousands of metres high, cover the ground with lava and ash, create devastating mud flows, bury and burn buildings, and even change the world's climate.

Case study: Heimaey

In January 1973 a split appeared on the island of Heimaey near Iceland.

Volcanic eruption

Fountains of lava poured from the split. Cinders rained down, forming huge cones, and lava flowed across the landscape, forming new rocks and enlarging the island by about a quarter of its original size. The eruption lasted five months. The town of Vestmannaeyjar was evacuated, and a third of its houses were destroyed, but people moved back afterwards.

Ground cracks

Landslides set off; giant waves form at sea

The landscape is changed

Lava and ash erupt

New mountains and islands form; mud flows occur

INSIDE THE EARTH

Before we can understand how earthquakes and volcanoes change the Earth's landscape we need to know about the structure of the Earth.

Inside In the centre of the Earth is the core, which is made mostly of iron. This is divided into the inner core and outer core. Around the core is the mantle. On top of the mantle is a very thin layer called the crust, which makes up the Earth's surface.

inner core   outer core   mantle   crust

crust

lithosphere

asthenosphere

Under the surface The top layers of the mantle are called the asthenosphere and the lithosphere. They are made up of hot, partly molten rock. These layers are responsible for creating earthquakes and volcanoes.

The crust, made of solid rock, rests on top of the lithosphere. The part that makes up the continents, called continental crust, is about 50 kilometres thick on average. The crust under the oceans, called ocean crust, is about 5 kilometres thick on average.

The huge pressure from the crust stops the incredibly hot rock in the mantle from turning to liquid.

Follow it through: plate movement

Heat is created in the Earth's core

Heat creates currents in semi-molten rock in the mantle

The cracked crust

The crust and the upper part of the lithosphere are cracked into huge pieces called tectonic plates. These plates float on top of the semi-molten rock underneath. They move at about the same speed as your fingernails grow. Scientists think that tectonic plates move because of the slow, swirling movements of semi-molten rock deep in the mantle.

Continental drift

The movements of the tectonic plates mean that some continents are moving apart and some are moving towards each other. This process, known as continental drift, has been going on for hundreds of millions of years. Two hundred million years ago, when dinosaurs lived on Earth, there was just one huge continent. Plate movements have split it into the continents we know today.

In the process new oceans have been created, old oceans have disappeared, and new mountain ranges, such as the Andes, have been built as continents have collided. Continental drift will carry on for millions of years to come, very gradually changing the look of the Earth's surface..

Take it further

The supercontinent of 200 million years ago was called Pangaea.

◆ Find a map of Pangaea.
◆ From an atlas, copy the outlines of North America, South America, Africa, India, the rest of Asia, Europe, Antarctica and Australia.
◆ Can you fit these shapes together to make the shape of Pangaea?

The great mountain chain of the Andes was built up by volcanic activity caused by movements of the tectonic plates.

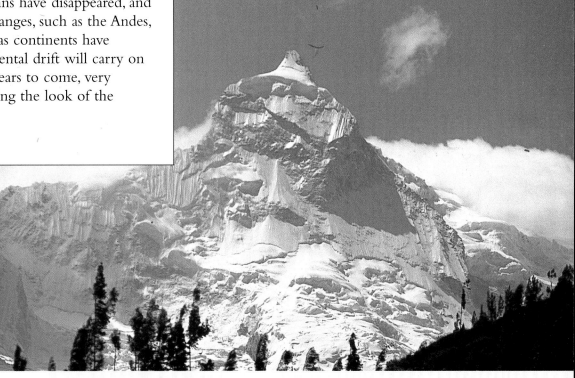

Currents flow along under the crust

Currents make the tectonic plates slowly move

Some continents move apart and some move towards each other

PLATE BOUNDARIES

The line where two tectonic plates meet is called a boundary. Most earthquakes and volcanoes happen at or near these boundaries. There are three main types of plate boundary, where plates are moving apart, moving towards each other or moving along each other.

A slice through the crust showing a constructive boundary and destructive boundaries

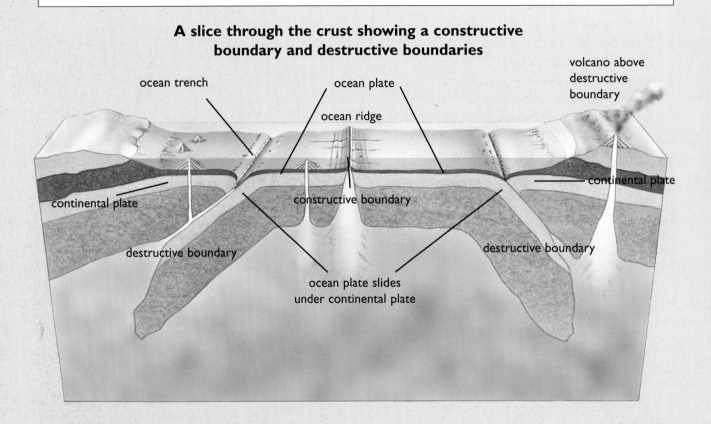

ocean trench

ocean plate

ocean ridge

volcano above destructive boundary

continental plate

constructive boundary

continental plate

destructive boundary

destructive boundary

ocean plate slides under continental plate

Destructive boundaries

A place where the edges of two plates are moving towards each other is called a destructive boundary, also called a subduction zone. When two plates meet, there are different effects depending on whether the plates make up a continent or are under the ocean.

Where a continental plate and an ocean plate meet, the ocean plate slides underneath the continental plate. It plunges into the mantle and melts, forming new magma.

Where two ocean plates meet, one plate slides under the other and melts. Where two continental plates collide, the plates crumple into each other, pushing up huge mountain ranges. The Himalayas were made when the Indian plate collided with the Asian plate.

Constructive boundaries

A place where the edges of two plates are moving away from each other is called a constructive boundary. As the plates move apart magma, which is molten rock from the mantle, flows up into the gap. The magma cools and hardens to form a new crust.

The Mid-Atlantic Ridge is a constructive boundary that runs north-south on the ocean floor of the Atlantic. The two plates are gradually moving apart, so the Atlantic is gradually getting wider. The Great Rift Valley in Africa is also a constructive boundary.

Take it further

Find a map of the ocean floor in an atlas.

◆ Can you identify the Mid-Atlantic Ridge (a constructive boundary)?
◆ Which island has formed over this spreading ridge?
◆ Look for other spreading ridges under other oceans.

A constructive boundary between two continental plates in Iceland. The line shows were the two plates are slowly moving apart.

Conservative boundaries

In some places the edges of two plates slide past each other, without moving apart or towards each other. No rock is made or destroyed, so this sort of boundary is called a conservative boundary. However, the movements break up the edges of the plates.

WHERE VOLCANOES HAPPEN

A volcano is simply a place where magma leaks out through a hole or crack in the Earth's crust. Most volcanoes happen along the constructive boundaries or destructive boundaries between tectonic plates, but a few happen far from plate boundaries.

Volcanoes at destructive boundaries

When an ocean plate plunges under another plate the ocean plate rubs against the plate above and it heats up. The rock melts, making magma under the upper plate. This pool of magma forces its way up through weak points in the crust. This creates a line of volcanoes parallel to the boundary, but off to one side in the upper plate.

Over millions of years the volcanoes create mountain ranges such as the Andes, or chains of islands such as the Aleutian Islands in the north Pacific. Most of the world's volcanoes happen at destructive boundaries.

Pacific Ocean

Mid-Atlantic Ridge

Great Rift Valley

Pacific Ocean

Atlantic Ocean

⌒ Plate boundary

▲ Active volcano

Earthquake zone

Most volcanoes (and earthquakes) happen on or near tectonic plate boundaries.

Follow it through: volcanic eruption

An ocean plate and a continental plate meet

The ocean plate sinks under the continental plate

Friction and pressure on the ocean plate

The Ring of Fire Nearly all the way round the Pacific Ocean is a line of destructive plate boundaries where ocean plates slide under continental plates and other ocean plates. These boundaries have created a circle of volcanoes around the rim of the Pacific known as the Ring of Fire. It runs up the west coasts of South America and North America, through the Aleutian Islands, through Japan, the Philippines and New Zealand.

Volcanoes at constructive boundaries Volcanoes also happen along constructive boundaries. As the two plates at the boundary move apart, magma wells up from underneath to fill the gap, forming volcanoes. We can think of the Mid-Atlantic Ridge that runs along the floor of the Atlantic as a continuous volcano thousands of kilometres long.

Hot-spot volcanoes Volcanoes also erupt thousands of kilometres away from tectonic plate boundaries. It is thought that these happen over places in the mantle that are hotter than normal. Magma from these 'hot spots' forces its way through the crust above.

All over the world There are about 500 volcanoes in the world that have erupted in the recent past, and on average 25 volcanoes erupt every year. A few have been erupting ever since people can remember.

Nyamulgaria in Congo, Africa is a hot-spot volcano.

| The ocean plate melts, making magma | Magma forces its way towards the surface | Magma breaks through the continental plate | A volcano erupts at the surface |

INSIDE A VOLCANO

Volcanoes come in many different shapes and sizes. The simplest volcano is just a crack in the ground that magma flows from. The biggest volcanoes are immense heaps of rock thousands of metres high. They are built up from layers of material that have been ejected during eruptions.

ash cloud

vent

side vent

lava flow

crust

magma chamber

Volcano parts The diagram shows the parts of a composite volcano (see page 19). Magma forces its way from the magma chamber, through the crust, then up the centre of the volcano through the hole in the top called the vent. A wide hole in the top of a volcano is also known as a crater. Magma sometimes comes out of side vents too.

Eruption products Magma is a mixture of molten rock and gases such as carbon dioxide and steam. Huge pressure on the magma when it is deep underground keeps the gas dissolved despite the high temperature. But when the magma rises through a volcano's vent, the pressure is released and the gas turns into bubbles. The gas comes out of the vent along with bits of molten rock called lava.

If small lumps of lava cool before they land they form small pieces of rock called cinders. Larger pieces are called volcanic bombs. Lava that lands while it is still molten forms red-hot liquid on the ground. In explosive eruptions the rock in magma can be turned into tiny fragments that cool quickly to form ash.

Take it further

Open a bottle of fizzy drink. Hold the bottle over the sink and make sure the top is pointing away from your face. Unscrew the cap very slowly and watch the liquid carefully.

◆ Why do you think bubbles appear in the liquid?
◆ Think how this relates to magma moving up to a volcano's vent.

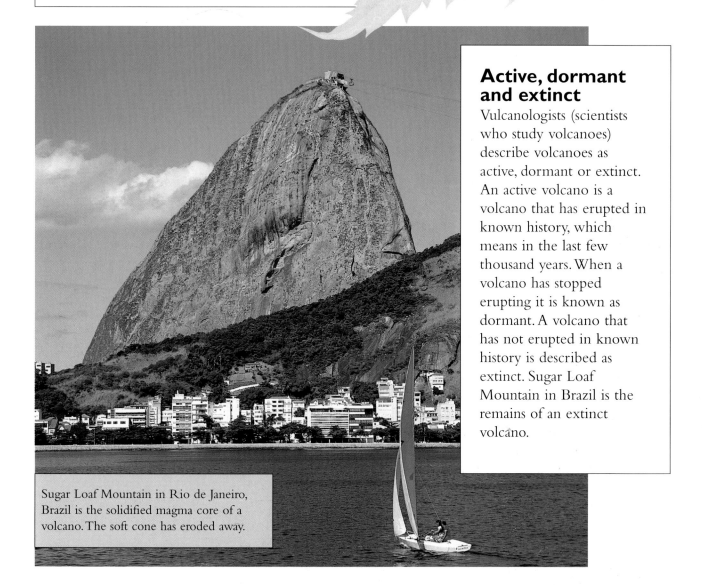

Sugar Loaf Mountain in Rio de Janeiro, Brazil is the solidified magma core of a volcano. The soft cone has eroded away.

Active, dormant and extinct

Vulcanologists (scientists who study volcanoes) describe volcanoes as active, dormant or extinct. An active volcano is a volcano that has erupted in known history, which means in the last few thousand years. When a volcano has stopped erupting it is known as dormant. A volcano that has not erupted in known history is described as extinct. Sugar Loaf Mountain in Brazil is the remains of an extinct volcano.

Volcanoes create new rocks that form part of the landscape. This is an important stage in the process called the rock cycle, in which new rocks are continually formed and old rocks are broken down and destroyed.

New rocks Molten rock from the magma released by the volcano cools and solidifies to form new rock. This often builds into mountains and mountain ranges (see page 18). Eruptions under the sea form a new ocean crust and even whole islands (see page 20).

Gentle eruptions The volcanoes that erupt at constructive boundaries and over hot spots tend to be gentle compared to the violent eruptions of some volcanoes. In these gentler eruptions lava comes out of the volcanoes in fountains. Such eruptions are known as Hawaiian and Strombolian eruptions after the islands where they were first studied.

The lava is driven out of the vent by gases released from the magma. It falls to the ground and forms pools. If the ground is sloping, the lava flows away from the vent in a river called a lava flow.

An eruption at Stromboli, near Sicily in Italy. The red-hot lava will cool to form new rock.

Follow it through: rock cycle

Lava flows from the volcano

Lava cools to form new igneous rock

Rock is eroded

Temperature or pressure changes

Rock formation

As soon as lava leaves a volcano vent it begins to cool. However, a deep lava flow can travel dozens of kilometres before it cools enough to stop flowing. Very runny lava can flow at up to 20 kilometres per hour on steep slopes. When the lava cools fully it forms igneous rock. Examples of igneous rocks from volcanoes are basalt, granite, andesite and pumice stone.

The other types of rock, sedimentary and metamorphic, are both ultimately formed from igneous rock. Sedimentary rock, such as sandstone and limestone, is created through compressed fragments of other rock and shells. Metamorphic rock is changed from its original state into a different rock due to changes in temperature and pressure.

Lava shapes

Small flows of very hot lava form rock with a surface like coiled rope. This is called pahoehoe lava. Large flows of cooler lava form rock with a sharp, jumbled surface. This is called aa (see page 7). Pahoehoe and aa are Hawaiian words.

A flow of pahoehoe lava formed this rock called basalt about 18,000 years ago.

Case study: the Deccan Traps, India

Sometimes lava flows spread out to form extensive lava fields that cover the landscape. One of the world's biggest lava fields is the Deccan Traps in India. It is also one of the largest volcanic features on Earth.

Thick layer

The Deccan Traps were formed about 65 million years ago, when lava flows created a layer of basalt, which was 2,000 metres thick, across an area of 500,000 square kilometres. Much of the basalt has been eroded away. Scientists think gases and ash from the eruption may have contributed to the extinction of the dinosaurs.

Layers of sediment form, which becomes sedimentary rock

Rock becomes metamorphic rock

Millions of years of rock movements

Rock moves deep underground

Rock melts to form magma

NEW MOUNTAINS

Lava and ash from volcanoes build into new hills and mountains thousands of metres high. A new volcanic hill or mountain may take millions of years to form or it can be created in just a few months or even a few days. The sort of volcanic hill or mountain formed depends on the type of eruption.

The Mauna Loa volcano in Hawaii is a shield volcano.

Shield volcanoes When very hot, runny lava is ejected from a volcano and spreads quickly across the landscape, it forms thin layers of new rock. Each eruption creates a new layer of rock on top of the previous one. Gradually a wide dome of rock is built up. This sort of volcano is known as a shield volcano because it is shaped like a curved shield lying on the ground. It looks like an upside-down dinner plate. The Mauna Loa volcano in Hawaii is an example of a shield volcano.

Follow it through: composite volcanoes

Magma moves upwards from under the crust

Pressure on the magma is reduced

Gas blasts lava into the air

A series of ash and cinder cones have built up on the island of Maui, Hawaii.

Cinder cones

Cinder cones Some volcanoes spew out magma that is about half gas, half lava. The gas expands as the magma rises to the surface. It throws small lumps of gas-filled lava high into the air. The lumps cool before they land, forming cinders. When the cinders land they form a cone-shaped hill with a wide crater in the top. This sort of volcano is called a cinder cone. Cinder cones often form in clusters and on the sides of larger volcanoes.

Composite volcanoes

Magma that contains a high percentage of gas and only a little lava tends to be ejected explosively, forming small particles of ash. A composite volcano, also known as a stratovolcano, is made up of layers of this ash with layers of lava in between. Some of these volcanoes form perfect cones thousands of metres high, such as Mount Fuji, Japan. These volcanoes form over destructive boundaries.

Case study: Paricutín, a new Mexican mountain

On 20 February 1943, Mexican farmer Dionisio Pulido noticed small earth tremors, and the ground in his fields felt warm. They were the first signs of a new volcano.

Eruption

The next day a crack opened in the ground and an eruption began. Ash soon began to pile into a cone, and lava flowed from the top and down the sides. By July a composite cone volcano, 300 metres high, dominated the landscape. Dionisio's village, Paricutín, had been buried. The eruption stopped in 1952 when the cone had reached 420 metres.

Lava cools to form ash	Ash piles up to form a cone	Fresh lava flows over the cone	More ash falls on the lava flows	A composite cone is built up

ISLAND BUILDING

There are many more volcanoes under the ocean than there are on the continents. Underwater eruptions happen at constructive boundaries such as the Mid-Atlantic Ridge, at destructive boundaries where two ocean plates meet, and over hot spots under the ocean. We never see most of these volcanoes, but some grow large enough to break the surface and form new islands.

Islands in constructive zones At constructive zones magma comes up between plates that are spreading apart. It cools very quickly to form rounded heaps of lava called pillow lava. In a few places such eruptions are large enough to build up whole islands. For example, Iceland was formed from lava flowing from the Mid-Atlantic Ridge.

Hot-spot islands On volcanic hot spots under the ocean floor, magma can force its way through the crust and form a shield volcano on the sea bed. If the eruption continues long enough, the tip of the volcano eventually forms a new island.

The island of Hawaii is the tip of a sea bed volcano. It is more than 9,000 metres high and 600 kilometres wide at its base. One of the volcanoes on Hawaii, Mauna Loa, is the world's most active volcano.

To the north-west of Hawaii is a line of islands formed from extinct volcanoes. It is thought that these all formed over the same hot spot as Hawaii.

The island of Hawaii seen from space. The whole island is made of material spewed from its volcanoes.

Follow it through: island chains

Hot magma under an ocean plate forms a hot spot

A volcano begins to form on the ocean floor

Eventually a volcano breaks the surface

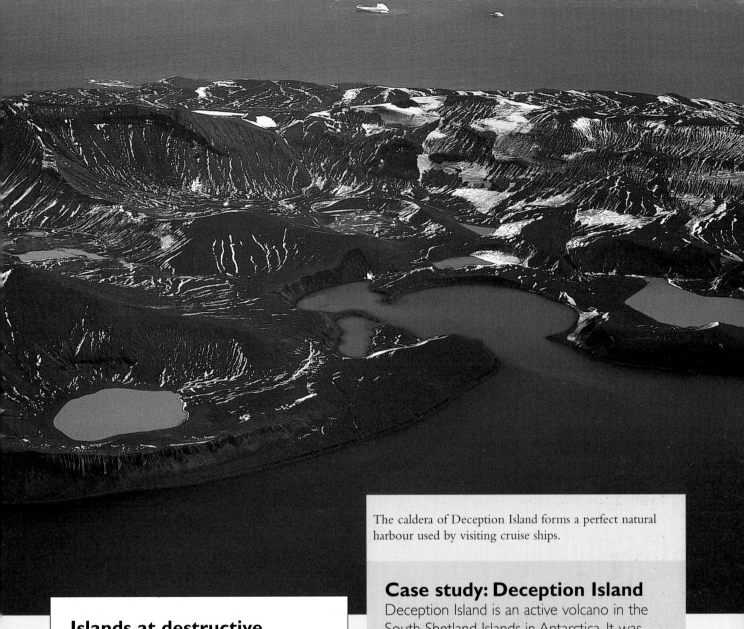

The caldera of Deception Island forms a perfect natural harbour used by visiting cruise ships.

Islands at destructive boundaries

Chains of volcanic islands form next to destructive boundaries. For example, a 3000-kilometre long chain of islands runs through the Pacific south of Japan. This is to the west of the Pacific plate where it slides under the Philippines plate. To the east of the islands is a trench in the ocean floor, up to 11,000 metres deep, where the Pacific plate dips down.

Case study: Deception Island

Deception Island is an active volcano in the South Shetland Islands in Antarctica. It was formed over a destructive boundary.

Caldera formation

Some time in the past Deception Island had a volcanic mountain in its centre. Then there was a catastrophic eruption that blew the mountain apart. The centre of the volcano collapsed into the magma chamber underneath and the sea rushed in, forming a caldera (see page 23). There have been minor eruptions during the last hundred years.

| A new island is formed | An ocean plate moves | The eruption stops | A new volcano begins to form in a different place on the sea bed | A chain of islands is formed |

EXPLOSIVE VOLCANOES

Eruptions of volcanoes over destructive boundaries are often extremely violent and spectacular. Instead of forming new rock or building new mountains these volcanoes can destroy themselves in huge explosions. They also change the landscape for many kilometres around. Explosive eruptions like this are called Plinian eruptions after Pliny, a Roman who saw the eruption of Vesuvius, Italy in 79CE.

Building up pressure The magma formed at destructive boundaries is thick and stiff, and contains a high percentage of gases. After an eruption in a volcano above a destructive boundary, the volcano's vent can become plugged with magma, preventing more magma from escaping.

Over many years, perhaps hundreds of years, more magma is forced into the magma chamber underneath the volcano. The pressure on the plug increases. Eventually the pressure becomes so large that the magma bursts out.

An example of a Plinian eruption. This is Mount Pinatubo in the Philippines at the height of its eruption in 1991.

Exploding out With the pressure on the magma released, the gases dissolved in it explode. The huge forces blow the lava in the magma into tiny pieces that cool to form ash. The top of the volcano cone can be blown apart, too. Explosive eruptions continue until the pressure in the magma chamber is reduced.

Calderas When the eruptions die down the top of the volcano can collapse into the empty magma chamber, forming a huge crater called a caldera. This often fills with water and a caldera lake is created. Crater Lake in Oregon, USA is a famous lake-filled caldera. It is about 10 kilometres wide and 1,000 metres deep.

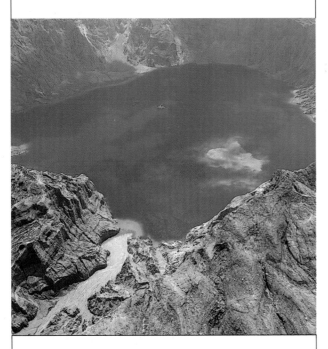

A caldera created by the eruption of Mount Pinatubo.

Rebuilding the cone After an explosive eruption destroys the top of a volcano, the volcano often begins to rebuild itself. Small eruptions of lava emerge from cracks in the volcano and form domes in the top of the volcano and down its sides.

The landscape around Mount St Helens was devastated after its eruption.

Case study: Mount St Helens, USA

Mount St Helens in the Rocky Mountains is a destructive boundary volcano.

Eruption

It had been dormant for more than 100 years when it erupted in 1980. The eruption began with ash and rock flying into the air. Then the north side of the mountain began to bulge. On 18 May the pressure inside caused the mountainside to collapse and there was a massive explosion of trapped gas.

Widespread destruction

Trees up to 30 kilometres away were broken like matchsticks. Valleys, lakes, and rivers were filled with mud and debris and vast numbers of animals, birds, and fish were killed, as well as 59 people. The top 400 metres of the mountain was blown away. A new cone is forming inside the vast crater that was left.

VOLCANIC ASH

The effect of a volcanic eruption is not limited to the volcano itself. Explosive eruptions can change the landscape for hundreds of kilometres around, and sometimes the whole of the Earth's surface.

Ash clouds Explosive eruptions create vast clouds of volcanic ash. The ash is carried into the air by hot gases rising upwards, just as smoke rises from a bonfire. Volcanic ash clouds can rise as far as 50 kilometres into the atmosphere. The ash gradually falls back to the ground, covering it in a thick grey blanket. This layer of ash is not light like dust, but as heavy as rock.

Mount Augustine in Alaska is a typical explosive volcano. In 1986, eruptions continued for several weeks, throwing up a permanent ash cloud 4,500 metres high. Occasional huge explosions pushed the ash cloud as high as 12,200 metres. The ash was thrown upwards from the explosions and carried still higher by the hot gases.

Ash exploding high into the air from Mount Augustine volcano, USA.

Follow it through: climate change

An explosive volcano creates clouds of ash

Ash is carried into the stratosphere by rising hot gas

High-level winds move the ash

24

Climate change The biggest explosive eruptions send ash into upper atmosphere, from where it spreads right around the Earth, carried by currents of air called the jet stream. This ash reduces the sunlight that can reach the Earth's surface. The eruption in 1815 of volcano Tambora in Indonesia is thought to have cut out so much light that crops failed all over the world.

Thick layers of ash found in sediments seem to show that there have been even more catastrophic eruptions in the distant past. These eruptions may have caused long-term cooling of the atmosphere, changing the world's climate, which in turn may have changed the pattern of plant and animal life, and even caused mass extinction to some types of wildlife.

Take it further

Search the Internet for videos of pyroclastic flows.

◆ Can you see how the heavy ash cloud flows down the hillside like an avalanche?
◆ Try to find examples filmed at night that show the glowing ash and rocks carried by the flow.

Pyroclastic flows Sometimes the ash cloud is so thick that rising gas cannot carry it upwards and away from the volcano. Instead it collapses and flows down the volcano's slopes like an avalanche. This is called a pyroclastic flow. It is made up of scorching hot gas and ash. Pyroclastic flows can reach speeds of more than 150 kilometres per hour, destroying everything in their path.

Central Luzon in the Philippines. The explosion of Mount Pinatubo covered the landscape in thick white ash. The volcano also emitted sulphur gases which may have contributed to climate change and damage to the ozone layer.

| A layer of ash is carried right around Earth | Ash blocks sunlight from reaching the surface | Less heat reaches the surface | The atmosphere cools | The world's climates are affected |

MUD, WAVES AND WATER

Mixing water with volcanoes can have devastating effects. Water and volcanic ash form rivers of mud, and explosive eruptions on islands can create huge waves at sea. Where water seeps into volcanically active ground, however, it creates interesting effects such as hot springs.

Mud flowing after the eruption of Mount Pinatubo, Philippines.

Mud flows

Ash deposits from volcanoes often mix with rain water or melted snow from a volcano's summit to create mud flows known as lahars. These sweep downhill into river valleys and follow the path of the rivers. The mud is incredibly dense. It carries away anything in its path, such as trees, bridges and buildings. When the flow finally comes to a stop the mud sets like a layer of concrete over the landscape.

Case study 1: Nevado del Ruiz mud slide, Colombia

In 1985 Nevado del Ruiz, a snow-capped volcano in the Andes in northern Columbia, began to erupt. The eruption was quite small, but the ash from pyroclastic flows melted snow and ice, forming lahars.

Devastating effects

The lahars flowed at speeds of up to 60 kilometres an hour. They eroded soil and loose rock and stripped vegetation. With the rock, vegetation and water from river channels, the lahars grew in size, becoming as thick as 50 metres in parts. Two and a half hours after the start of the eruption one of the lahars reached the town of Armero, which was 74 kilometres from the explosion crater. In a few minutes the town was buried forever under many metres of mud, along with 22,000 of its inhabitants, around three-quarters of the population.

Volcano waves

Explosive eruptions of island volcanoes can leave vast craters in the sea. The sea rushes to fill the crater, creating monster waves called tsunamis. You can find out about the effects of tsunamis on page 37. In 1883 the Indonesian island of Krakatoa blew up, leaving a crater 290 metres deep in the sea floor. The tsunamis created were up to 40 metres high and killed about 36,000 people on nearby islands.

Follow it through: mud flows

Volcano erupts

Heat from lava melts snow and ice

Heavy rain falls

Water mixes with ash to make mud

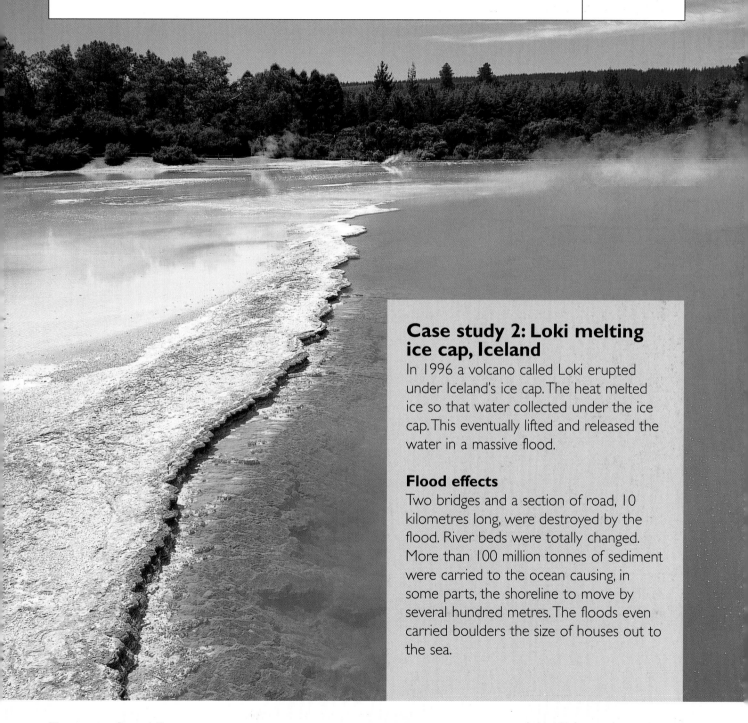

Volcanic features There are often peculiar features on the landscape on and around volcanoes. The rocks under the ground are heated by magma close by. Hot springs often flow from these hot rocks. In a few places water boils quickly underground and the steam throws columns of water back up, forming geysers. Hot rock also forms pools of boiling volcanic mud.

A multi-coloured steaming mud pool at Waiotapu Thermal Park, North Island, New Zealand.

Case study 2: Loki melting ice cap, Iceland

In 1996 a volcano called Loki erupted under Iceland's ice cap. The heat melted ice so that water collected under the ice cap. This eventually lifted and released the water in a massive flood.

Flood effects

Two bridges and a section of road, 10 kilometres long, were destroyed by the flood. River beds were totally changed. More than 100 million tonnes of sediment were carried to the ocean causing, in some parts, the shoreline to move by several hundred metres. The floods even carried boulders the size of houses out to the sea.

Torrents of mud flow into river valleys

Mud flows onto flood plains

Mud slows, stops and sets hard

All the effects volcanoes bring to the natural landscape also affect features created by humans. For example, lava flows bury farmland, burn buildings and block roads, thick ash deposits bury homes, and mud flows carry away bridges and destroy towns.

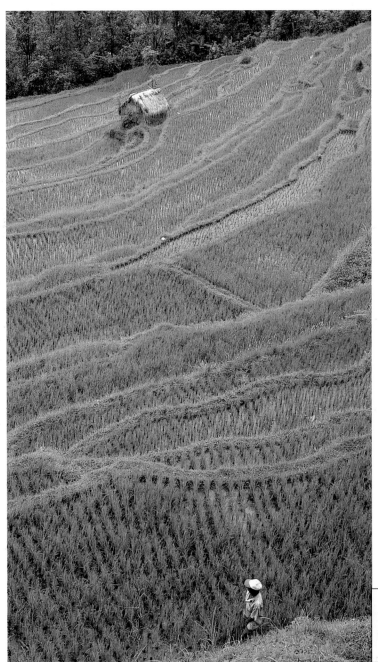

Living with volcanoes

Despite this, about one in ten of the world's population (about 600 million people) lives in cities, towns and villages where they are at risk from eruptions.

The people most likely to be at risk are farmers in less economically developed countries. Crops grow very well near volcanoes because the soil, formed from lava and volcanic ash, is rich in minerals. In some places farmers even build terraced fields on the steep volcano slopes.

Towns and cities have also been built near volcanoes, often because of lack of space elsewhere. Generally, people accept the risks of living near volcanoes because the chances of being hurt are small and the advantages outweigh the risks.

With the increasing number of people on Earth more people will be forced to move into dangerous volcanic regions.

Rice terraces thrive on volcanic ash at Mount Agung in Bali, Indonesia.

Permanent and temporary changes

Sometimes places are permanently changed by volcanic eruptions and their effects. For example, lava and mud flows can bury farmland and communities for good. Then people are forced to move on. But often ash can be removed, lava flows can be cleared from roads, and people can return to their homes and lives. A few years later there may be no sign that an eruption ever took place.

The city of Quito in Ecuador lies in a valley surrounded by volcanoes. It regularly receives a covering of volcanic ash. In 2002, an eruption of the volcano El Reventador dropped five centimetres of ash on the city. Local people are well prepared for these events. They formed teams to collect and carry away the ash, and the city was working again within a few days.

Human effects

Gentle eruptions are not normally dangerous because lava flows quite slowly and there is plenty of time to escape. But violent eruptions can be deadly. People close to volcanoes can be caught in ash falls, pyroclastic flows, mudslides and tsunamis.

When the composite volcano, Vesuvius, erupted in Italy in 79CE it buried the towns of Herculaneum and Pompeii under many metres of ash. When it erupted again in 1944 the ruins of Pompeii were buried under ash once again, but this was only temporary.

Plaster casts of the people overcome by volcanic ash in the streets of Pompeii in 79CE.

Case study: Mount Pinatubo, Philippines

The Philippines is a less economically developed country, with a relatively high population. In 1991, Mount Pinatubo erupted after being dormant for 400 years.

Widespread effects

Earth tremors were felt in April and the mountain's sides began to swell. A series of explosions in June sent up an ash cloud 20 kilometres high. Ash fell to the ground, turning farmland for 50 kilometres around into wasteland and burying more than 40,000 homes. Despite mass evacuations thousands of people died in collapsed homes, pyroclastic flows and mudslides (see page 26).

An earthquake happens when rocks in the Earth's crust move suddenly, creating shaking on the Earth's surface. The shaking causes changes to the landscape such as cracks in the ground and landslides, and, if strong enough, it can destroy buildings. About 10,000 earthquakes are felt every year, most of which are so small they are detected only by sensitive instruments.

Slipping plates
1 Two plates catch as they grind against each other.

Slipping plates Like volcanoes, most earthquakes happen on or near the boundaries between the Earth's tectonic plates (see map page 12).

Tectonic plates grind past each other rather than sliding smoothly. As one plate moves against the other, it can catch. The edges of the plates stop moving, but pressure gradually builds as the rest of the plate keeps going, bending, stretching and squashing the rocks at the edges.

At some point the pressure becomes too large and the catch releases. The plates move suddenly, releasing the pressure, then catch again. This sudden jerk causes an earthquake.

2 Pressure builds up until eventually the catch releases, causing an earthquake.

Follow it through: earthquakes

Tectonic plates move past each other

The surfaces of the plate edges stop moving

The plates keep moving

Destructive and conservative quakes

Major earthquakes happen at both destructive and conservative boundaries. At destructive boundaries earthquakes can come from almost any depth, and the movements of the rocks are often large.

At conservative boundaries the movement of the plates past each other fractures the two plate edges, creating a band of faults – cracks in rock – up to 100 kilometres across. Earthquakes that happen at conservative boundaries tend to come from near the surface.

Surface evidence

Some faults are deep below ground but some are near the surface. Some go right through the crust. Often the rocks on each side of a fault have moved up, down or sideways.

The San Andreas fault in the USA is on a conservative boundary. Here the two plates are actually both moving in the same direction, but one is moving faster than the other, which causes break-up.

The San Andreas fault runs for about 950 kilometres along the coast of California.

More earthquake zones

Earthquakes are also caused by the movement of magma at constructive boundaries and under volcanoes, and where continental plates collide and scrunch together, pushing up mountain ranges.

They can also happen far from plate boundaries, in places we would not expect them. Such earthquakes are probably caused by faults formed millions of years ago.

The British Isles are thousands of kilometres from any plate boundary, but experience minor earthquakes. In 2002 an earthquake centred in the Midlands was felt up to 100 kilometres around. It was caused by movement in an ancient fault deep underground.

| Pressure builds on rock at the plate edges | Rocks bend, compact and stretch | The catch releases | Rocks spring back into shape | An earthquake is set off |

EARTHQUAKE WAVES

The point in the Earth's crust where two plates slip and create an earthquake is called the focus. Energy, released from the pressurised rocks, radiates out from the focus in shock waves called seismic waves.

Body waves The seismic waves that spread out through the Earth from the focus are called body waves. They spread out in all directions – both towards the surface and deeper into the Earth. They travel many kilometres every second.

Two types of body waves are given out – primary and secondary. Primary waves move in waves of compression and tension, like sound passing through the air. Secondary waves move like a wave along a string, shaking the rocks from side to side.

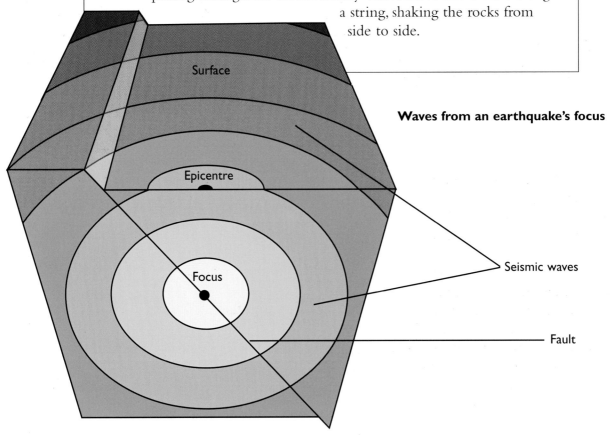

Waves from an earthquake's focus

Surface

Epicentre

Focus

Seismic waves

Fault

Follow it through: seismic waves

Rocks spring back into shape as a boundary or fault slips at the focus

The movement sets up body seismic waves

Surface waves When body waves reach the surface, they create waves that travel across the surface. There are two types of these surface waves: Rayleigh and Love waves, named after the scientists who first described them. Seismic waves make the landscape move up and down and from side to side as they pass, but normally leave it undamaged after they have gone.

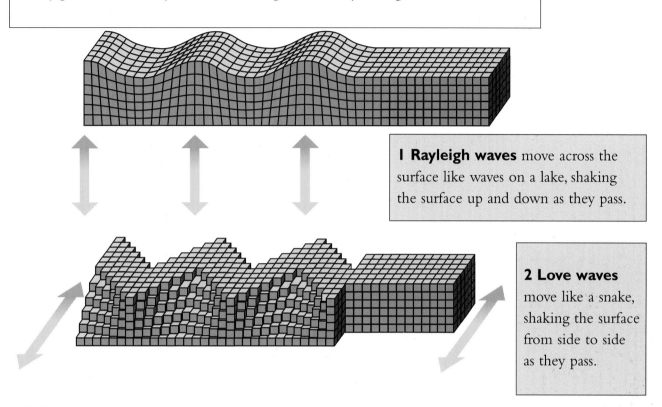

1 Rayleigh waves move across the surface like waves on a lake, shaking the surface up and down as they pass.

2 Love waves move like a snake, shaking the surface from side to side as they pass.

Earthquake scales The magnitude of an earthquake is a measure of the energy it releases. It is measured on the Richter Scale. On this scale a small earthquake might measure 3, a strong quake 6, and a massive quake 8 or more. Going up the scale by one represents an increase in energy of ten times.

The intensity of an earthquake is a measure of its strength based on the changes it causes to the landscape. It is normally measured on the Modified Mercalli Scale. On this scale level 1 is a minor tremor that causes no damage, and level 12 is total devastation.

Weakening waves As seismic waves spread out from the focus they get weaker, just as a sound gets quieter further from the source. So, although an earthquake can have only one magnitude, its intensity reduces as the distance from the focus increases.

The epicentre The greatest intensity is at the epicentre – the point on the surface directly above the focus. A medium magnitude earthquake with a shallow focus can be more intense, and cause more damage, than one with a high magnitude and a deep focus.

Body waves reach the surface

Surface waves are set up

Surface waves spread from the epicentre

Body waves and surface waves shake the ground

During an earthquake seismic waves shake the ground. There can also be small earthquakes before and after the main earthquake (called foreshocks and aftershocks). But this shaking is only temporary. So what are the lasting effects of earthquakes on the natural landscape?

Surface upheaval Strong seismic waves can rip layers of weak rock apart, creating cracks in the surface. These are normally just hairline cracks rather than wide chasms.

If the two sides of a fault move in an earthquake, the ground on one side can move up or down compared to the other. This creates a new step in the land called a scarp.

Sideways (or transverse) movements of faults rip the surface. These can be seen by a line of disturbed ground, or sections of road or fences that have moved out of line. An earthquake in Montana, USA in 1959 caused timber and road damage estimated at $11 million.

Streets cracked by ground waves during the 1959 Montana earthquake, USA.

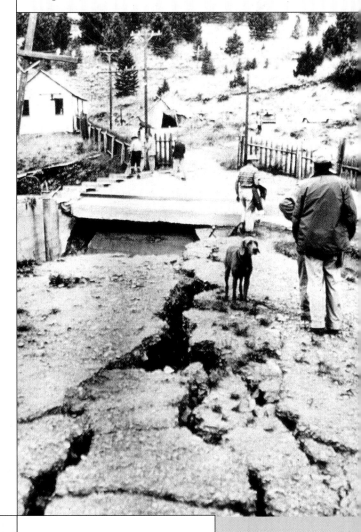

A raised beach in Cornwall, UK.

Raised beaches

Earthquakes can make the ground rise or fall by several metres, or be tilted. These changes are not always easy to see. Evidence for them comes from raised and sunken beaches. A raised beach is an eroded shoreline that has been lifted above sea level.

Backwards rivers Tilting ground can also make rivers change their course. In the early 1800s an earthquake in Tennessee, USA made the Mississippi River flow backwards, filling depressions in the land to create new lakes.

Landslides The shaking caused by earthquakes is often enough to make unstable hillsides, mountain slopes and cliffs fall downwards, creating a landslide. In a large landslide, soil and rock accelerate down the slope, sweeping away everything in their path. Landslides can fill valleys creating temporary dams which then collapse releasing flood water. Earthquakes also set off avalanches on snow slopes.

A strong earthquake in Ecuador in 1987 caused landslides that dumped millions of tonnes of soil into the River Amazon.

Case study: Peruvian landslide

In 1970 an earthquake with a magnitude of 7.7 struck off the coast of Peru.

Wide effects

Towns and villages 65 kilometres along the coast were badly damaged, but the worst devastation was 65 kilometres inland, in the heart of the Andes. Here the earthquake had triggered an immense landslide of snow and rock. It reached 280 kilometres per hour before spreading out 10 metres thick on the valley floor. The towns of Yungay and Ranrahirca were buried and 50,000 people lost their lives.

The combination of an earthquake and a landscape containing water can cause major problems. Ground that appears to be perfectly solid turns to quicksand. The shaking creates damaging waves on lakes, and worse still monster waves at sea.

Waterlogged soil

Land such as flood plains, coastal flats, old lake beds and reclaimed land is normally made up of layers of sediment such as silt and sand. In millions of years these will become new sedimentary rock, but until then they are soft and often waterlogged. Shaking these sediments has a strange effect on them. The water moves to the surface, creating quicksand. This is known as liquefaction. When the shaking stops the water sinks down and the ground turns solid again.

The effects of liquefaction

Liquefaction can have devastating consequences. Heavy objects resting on the ground sink downwards. Lighter things underground, such as underground pipes and even human bones, float upwards to the surface. If the ground is on a slope, the hillside turns to mud and forms a mudslide. New springs can emerge from the ground. Occasionally, water is ejected in fountains through weak spots in the surface. The water carries sand, which forms volcano-like cones several metres high.

During the 1964 Alaskan earthquake, soft clay liquefied and slid downhill.

Follow it through: tsunamis

| An earthquake under the ocean | The ocean floor moves up or down | Water above moves up or down |

Tsunamis If an earthquake happens in rocks under a sea or ocean, the shock waves disturb the water. If the ocean floor falls or rises suddenly as well, the water falls or rises too. These movements create huge waves called tsunamis that travel across the ocean. Landslides on coasts of continental shelves can set off waves too.

A tsunami starts off very low, with a long wavelength (a large distance between each crest) and travels up to 700 kilometres per hour. People on ships in mid-ocean do not even notice it passing.

But when the tsunami reaches shallow water it slows down, its wavelength reduces and its height grows. Strong tsunamis can grow as high as a ten-storey building. When a tsunami hits the shore it crashes inland, carrying boats and buildings with it.

Take it further

Investigate how liquefaction works.

◆ Put five tablespoons of cornflour into a bowl.
◆ Slowly add water until the mixture is a thick, sticky paste. Let the paste settle. Press the surface. Does it resist?
◆ Now shake your finger quickly from side to side as you press. Does the paste turn to a liquid? This is how ground liquefies in an earthquake.

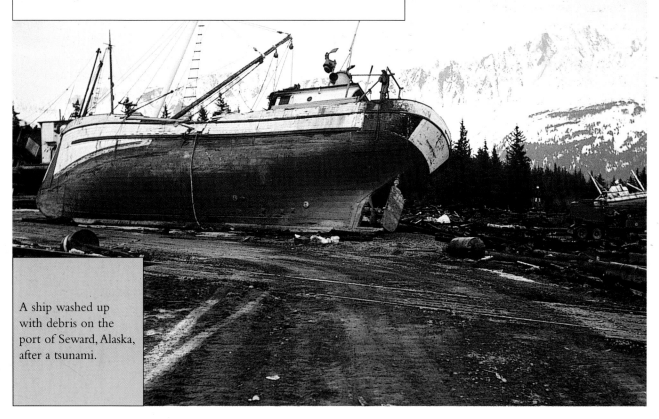

A ship washed up with debris on the port of Seward, Alaska, after a tsunami.

Waves spread from the epicentre

Waves travel fast across deep ocean

Waves get higher as they reach the shore

Water rushes inland

The landscape is flooded

COLLAPSING BUILDINGS

Seismologists (scientists who study earthquakes) often say that earthquakes do not kill people – buildings do. The vast majority of people killed and injured in earthquakes are trapped in buildings that topple or crumble because of the ground shaking underneath. In major earthquakes urban landscapes can be completely destroyed. Even buildings that stay standing may have to be later pulled down because of structural damage.

Earthquake damage in Kobe.

Why buildings collapse

As seismic waves pass a point on the ground, the ground moves violently up and down and from side to side. Up and down movements do not tend to damage buildings because buildings are designed to carry vertical forces. But sideways shaking can make all types of buildings collapse.

The walls of simple mud-brick houses are shaken to bits. Even concrete buildings can collapse like card houses.

The waves move up the building, cracking the joints between the concrete walls and floors, and the floors collapse on top of each other into a jumbled heap of concrete, brick and dust.

Case study: the Kobe earthquake, Japan

In January 1995 Kobe was hit by an earthquake measuring 7.2 on the Richter Scale.

Earthquake damage

More than 6,000 people died and nearly 200,000 buildings collapsed or were damaged. Most modern buildings survived. A long section of a flyover toppled sideways, and subway tunnels collapsed. The worst affected area was in the centre of Kobe along the main docks and port. This area is built on soft and easily moved rocks and the port itself is built on reclaimed land. Here the ground liquefied (see page 36) so buildings fell sideways.

Fire damage

Many of the deaths and damage were caused by fires from broken gas mains. The collapse of electricity and telephone lines meant that it was difficult for the fire-teams to find out where the fires were. It took over two days to control the fires, by which time it is estimated that over 7,000 buildings were damaged and 500 people were killed by fire.

Follow it through: collapsing buildings

Waves spread

The ground shakes from side to side

Buildings shake from side to side

Buildings that survive

Whether a building survives depends on its structure, its height and how quickly the ground shakes. Tall buildings often survive better than buildings of medium height, even though they might sway wildly. Some tall buildings have collapsed because their tops have collided with each other.

Earthquake proofing

Buildings can be designed to withstand earthquakes. In most cities at risk from earthquakes new buildings must be earthquake proof. Making a building earthquake resistant is often as simple as making it stronger. For example, adding extra steel reinforcement to a concrete building can stop the concrete crumbling. It may not prevent a building being damaged beyond repair, but it may stop it collapsing completely. A building can also be isolated from the ground to minimise the shaking spreading into it. One way of achieving this is by mounting it on rubber foundations.

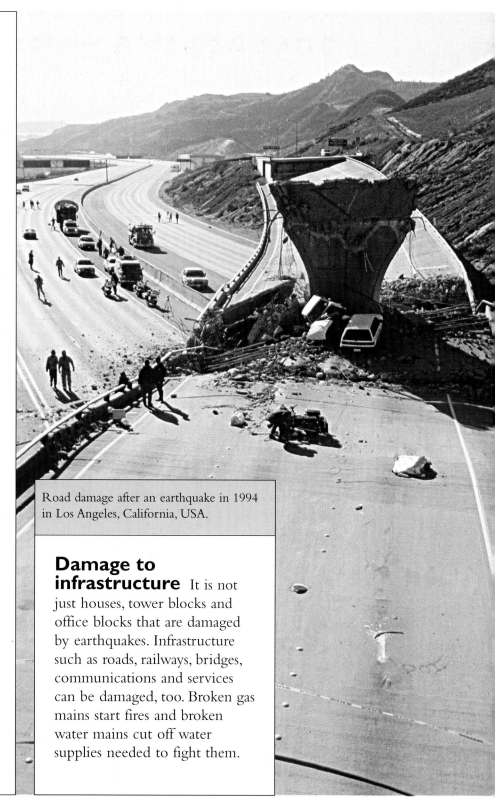

Road damage after an earthquake in 1994 in Los Angeles, California, USA.

Damage to infrastructure

It is not just houses, tower blocks and office blocks that are damaged by earthquakes. Infrastructure such as roads, railways, bridges, communications and services can be damaged, too. Broken gas mains start fires and broken water mains cut off water supplies needed to fight them.

Walls of brick buildings are shaken apart

The structure of concrete buildings is broken

Buildings collapse

People are trapped under rubble or concrete slabs

LIVING WITH EARTHQUAKES

Changes to urban landscapes caused by earthquakes are normally only temporary. After victims are found, rubble is quickly cleared away, buildings rebuilt and services restored. Only in ancient times were earthquake-damaged cities completely abandoned.

Tonnes of rubble must be painstakingly lifted in the search for earthquake survivors. This is a scene in Turkey in 1999.

Rich and poor

Clearing up after earthquakes, however, is an expensive process, and so happens more quickly in more economically developed countries than less economically developed countries, where people may have to live in temporary accommodation for many years.

About 30,000 people were killed and 500,000 more made homeless by a quake that hit the Indian state of Gujarat in 2001. Despite international aid, thousands of the homeless were still living in tented camps two years later.

Earthquake risks Hundreds of millions of people live in earthquake zones, many of them in major cities such as San Francisco, Tokyo and Istanbul. All these cities were hit by severe earthquakes in the 20th century. It is almost certain that they will be hit again this century, but they have been rebuilt and continue to grow. It is simply impractical to relocate these cities, and most people have little choice but to live in them.

Learning by mistakes

It is important for structural engineers to learn what goes wrong with buildings in earthquakes. They try to work out why buildings collapse so that poor designs can be avoided in future.

Unfortunately this does not always happen. For example, after a Turkish earthquake in 1999 engineers discovered that the builders of collapsed concrete tower blocks had taken shortcuts to save money on materials, making the buildings dangerously weak.

Be prepared

We cannot stop earthquakes happening, but we can reduce the risks to people by making sure that the inhabitants, authorities and emergency services are prepared. This can be as simple as telling people to take shelter under tables during an earthquake.

In urban areas of more economically developed countries, plans can be put into action within minutes. But in remote areas of less economically developed countries, victims may have to fend for themselves for days until help arrives.

Take it further

Look at a political map in an atlas.

◆ Compare the map to the earthquake location map on page 12.
◆ Can you identify major cities that are at risk from earthquakes?

Children practise an earthquake drill in California, USA. As well as regular drills the building is earthquake-resistant, with shatter-proof windows and an earthquake alarm. Computers and bookcases are bolted down to stop them falling.

EARTHQUAKE AND VOLCANO RESEARCH

Research into volcanoes (called vulcanology) and earthquakes (called seismology) is very important. Scientists try to understand why earthquakes and volcanoes happen and predict when they will occur. This is difficult because the causes of earthquakes and volcanoes are deep underground. However, monitoring tiny changes to the landscape can help.

A vulcanologist using a camera next to a lava flow on Mount Etna, on the Italian island of Sicily, Italy.

Monitoring volcanoes A volcano gives plenty of clues that it is about to erupt. For example, there are small earth tremors as magma begins to move, the ground swells as pressure builds up, and particular gases, such as sulphur dioxide, are emitted.

Vulcanologists use instruments such as seismometers to monitor these signs. Examining rock and ash around a volcano tells vulcanologists when previous eruptions happened and how long they lasted. Using this data they get an idea of the pattern of eruptions from a volcano, which helps with long-term predictions.

Monitoring earthquakes

Earthquakes are much harder to predict than volcanic eruptions. They tend to happen suddenly, without warning.

Seismologists use seismographs to monitor earthquakes, and other instruments to measure movements across faults. Readings tell them whether plate boundaries and rocks on each side of faults are moving past each other smoothly. If the movement stops for longer than normal, an earthquake is likely to follow – but it could be the next day or the next year.

Other signs of an impending earthquake are movements of water under the ground and changes in the electrical resistance of the rocks.

There is a network of seismographs all over the world. They are very sensitive and can detect earthquakes on the other side of the world. Data from them helps scientists to understand how seismic waves travel.

Warning and evacuation

If a volcanic eruption seems imminent, people at risk can be evacuated, although it is normally hard to predict an exact eruption time. This was successful in the case of the Mount Pinatubo eruption in 1991 and eruptions on Hawaii, where it was even possible to tell which vent magma would flow from.

There is normally no time to give earthquake warnings, and evacuating big cities in hours is impractical anyway. However, seismologists can say if a large earthquake is likely in the following years, and maps are drawn up to show which areas of cities are most at risk from building collapse.

In conclusion

Earthquakes and volcanoes are driven by huge forces produced deep inside the Earth. They have created sweeping changes to our natural landscape over millions of years, and will continue to do so.

We cannot stop earthquakes and volcanoes happening, but with research, predictions and warnings, we may be able to reduce both the changes they make to the human landscape and the number of people who lose their lives.

Case study: the Neptune Project

The Neptune Project is a joint scheme run by the USA and Canada to study the plates beneath the oceans.

Ocean observatory

The project involves the installation of 3,000 kilometres of fibre-optic cables linked to sensors across a plate under the Pacific Ocean. These will send real-time information about our changing planet via the internet to shore-based users. It will mean that the changes associated with earthquakes will be continually monitored and so help to prevent future disasters.

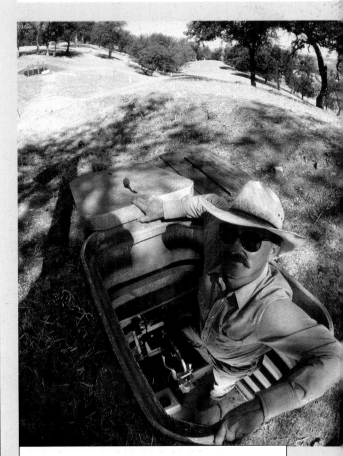

A technician checks a creepmeter at Parkfield in Central California. Creepmetres can detect ground movements of only 0.02 millimetres and can often give the first warning of an earthquake.

GLOSSARY

Ash — Tiny particles of rock thrown out of a volcano

Boundary — A place where two tectonic plates meet

Caldera — A huge crater, often full of water, formed when a volcano collapses into its magma chamber

Cinders — Small pieces of rock formed when lumps of lava ejected from a volcano cool before they land

Climate — The pattern of weather in a place over a long period of time

Conservative boundary — A plate boundary where two plates slide past each other

Constructive boundary — A plate boundary where two plates move apart and new crust is made

Crater — A dish-shaped hole in the top of a volcano

Crust — The rocky top layer of the Earth

Destructive boundary — A plate boundary where two plates move towards each other and crust is destroyed

Epicentre — The point on the Earth's surface directly above the focus of an earthquake

Eruption — Lava or ash coming from a volcano

Fault — A crack in the Earth's crust

Focus — The point in the Earth where an earthquake happens

Friction — The force that tries to stop two touching surfaces sliding past each other

Hot spot — A spot in a tectonic plate where magma forces its way through

Hot spring — A place where water heated by hot underground rocks flows out of the ground

Ice cap — A thick, permanent layer of ice on the top of a high mountain range or at the poles

Lahar — A mud flow made up of volcanic ash and water

Lava — Hot, molten rock that comes from a volcano

Magma — A mixture of molten rock and gases under the Earth's crust

Magma chamber — A huge cavern under a volcano full of magma

Mantle — The thick layer of hot rocks between the Earth's core and crust

Mass extinction — An event in which thousands of species of animal are killed off at the same time

Mid-Atlantic Ridge	A line of underwater mountains along a constructive boundary in the centre of the Atlantic Ocean
Pyroclastic flow	An avalanche of hot gas and ash that flows down the side of a volcano
Seismic waves	Waves that spread through the Earth and across the surface from the focus of an earthquake
Subterranean	Under the ground
Tectonic plates	The huge sections that the Earth's crust is cracked into
Tsunami	A giant ocean wave caused by an undersea earthquake, a landslide or volcanic explosion
Vent	A hole in a volcano from where lava or ash is emitted

FURTHER INFORMATION

British Geological Survey
The BGS earthquake site gives general information about earthquakes as well as up-to-date information on British earthquakes.

www.earthquakes.bgs.ac.uk

United States Geological Survey
The USGS site has the latest news on earthquakes around the world. Features an excellent education section.

www.earthquake.usgs.gov

Discovery Channel
The Discovery Channel earthquake site includes an earthquake simulator to play with.

http://tlc.discovery.com/convergence/quakes/interactives/makeaquake.html

Volcano World
Dedicated volcano website. Features plenty of volcano photos and videos, reports and stories.

http://volcano.und.edu

The Stromboli website
Excellent site mainly about the Stromboli volcano in Italy. Also features other Italian volcanoes, including Etna. Links to volcano webcams.

www.educeth.ch/stromboli/

Monserrat Volcano Observatory
Latest news, pictures and research from the Soufriere Hills volcano that has devastated the island of Monserrat in the Caribbean since 1995.

www.mvo.ms

Note to parents and teachers: Every effort has been made by the Publishers to ensure that these websites are suitable for children, that they are of the highest educational value, and that they contain no inappropriate or offensive material. However, because of the nature of the Internet, it is impossible to guarantee that the contents of these sites will not be altered. We strongly advise that Internet access is supervised by a responsible adult.

INDEX